SEEING YELLOW

First published in 2018 by
The Dedalus Press
13 Moyclare Road
Baldoyle
Dublin D13 K1C2
Ireland

www.dedaluspress.com

Copyright © Eva Bourke, 2018

ISBN 978 1 910251 37 9

All rights reserved.
No part of this publication may be reproduced in any form
or by any means without the prior permission
of the publisher.

The moral right of the author has been asserted.

Dedalus Press titles are represented in the UK by
Inpress Books, www.inpressbooks.co.uk,
and in North America by Syracuse University Press, Inc.,
www.syracuseuniversitypress.syr.edu.

Cover design: 'Treated decollage of Audubon bird study',
from the series *For the birds,* Benjamin de Burca, 2012

The Dedalus Press receives financial assistance from
The Arts Council / An Chomhairle Ealaíon.

SEEING YELLOW

EVA BOURKE

DEDALUS PRESS

ACKNOWLEDGEMENTS

Acknowledgements are due to the editors of the following publications where a number of these poems first appeared:

Poetry Ireland Review: 'Seeing Yellow', 'Jesus in Mayo', 'Sister Hildegard at 98 Considers her Life', 'Pietà', 'Small Railway Stations'; *The Irish Times:* 'Near Gare de l'Est', 'Fashions'; *Fermata: Writings Inspired by Music,* eds. V. Woods and E. Bourke; 'The Irish Tenor Michael Kelly Recalls Mozart in Paris','Riddle Canon'; *The Strokestown Anthology 2017,* ed. Paddy Bushe: 'Brooklyn Morning Weddings', *The Strokestown Anthology 2018,* ed. Margaret Hickey; 'Heimat'; *Watching my Hands at Work: Festschrift for Adrian Frazier,* ed. Louis de Paor, Megan Buckley and E. Bourke: 'Song'; *Southword,* ed. Matthew Sweeney: 'Summer with Juan Miró'; *The Clifden Anthology:* 'Trompe-l'Oeil'; *Even the Daybreak: 35 Years of Salmon Poetry,* ed. Jessie Lendennie: 'Berlin Nocturama'.

'Gallery' was commissioned by Janet McLean of the National Gallery Ireland and published in *Lines of Vision: Irish Writers on Art* (2014).

'If You Leave Letterfrack' was commissioned for the Letterfrack Poetry Trail and published in *A Trail of Thought,* Letterfack.

For Ono

CONTENTS

Gallery / 9
Catch of the Day / 11
Seeing Yellow / 12
My brother writes to me / 14
Lament for the Birds / 18
Near Gare de l'Est / 22
The Irish Tenor Michael Kelly Recalls
Mozart in Paris / 24
Riddle Canon / 26
Berlin Diary / 28
Forefathers / 31
Heimat / 33
By the River / 35
Fashions / 38
Paternoster / 40
Small Railway Stations / 43
Song / 45
Brooklyn Morning Weddings / 47
First Snow / 49
Oliphant Palace / 50
Still Lifes / 52
Wilderness / 53
Zoo / 55
Nocturama / 57
Lives / 58
Summer with Juan Miró / 60
Jesus in Mayo / 62
Sister Hildegard at 98 Considers Her Life / 64
Trompe-l'Oeil / 66

The China Shop Prepares for the Visit
of the Elephant / 67
Berlin Nocturama / 69
Pietà / 71
Hospital / 73
Bluebeard / 77
Questions of Grammar / 78
Disintegrating Love Poem Found on a Coffee Table
at the Berlin Poetry Festival / 80
Spring Dawn in the Old Part of Town / 84
Renvyle / 86
Before You Leave Letterfrack / 88
Plans / 89

Gallery

Quiet empty rooms,
the parquet floor creaked only under my feet
and all the food on the tables,

the knives, pewter plates, lobsters
and hams, grapes, overripe
and bursting with sweetness,

lay abandoned, just the curling lemon peel
still swayed a little. Tears of condensation ran
down the overturned wineglasses.

There was plenty for everyone
in the universe of colour, a banquet for all
the hungry, and time to eat it, more than enough.

***

Wilted petals, insects, partridge feathers
fell from the pages of my notebook and hare's
blood dripped through my hands.

***

The girl standing among scrubbed vessels dreamed
of something marvellous – something that
approached her on tiptoe and placed a hand on her shoulder.

***

A glint of light in the pupils of the man
holding an orange blossom; his love note was being read
by a woman in cold silks on the opposite wall.

***

I had come to see my ancestor stand before the ghetto wall,
   anno 1526.
His black velvet collar pulled up around his chin
he coughed into a blood-stained handkerchief.

The wall remains but who remembers him, his rank at court,
his services to the archduke? Pigeons muttered on the sills
and the archives of forgetting in the cellar rustled.

***

All tried to escape from the frames: children, men on horseback,
kitchen maids, even the snail by the angel's right foot who crept
the wrong way and missed the miracle,

and the young mother wished she could step out of her niche,
hand the baby across the sill to the custodian, for just a minute,
and shed the golden monstrosity that gave her headaches.

***

Clouds on their way towards a port just out of sight – Rotterdam
   perhaps,
a fleet of sailboats adrift on the surface of morning
carrying the news we had long been waiting for.

***

A pair of earrings, a drop of sun, windfall apples under trees,
a village in the crook of a river's arm,
all the round, painted earth.

Catch of the Day

At nightfall in the calm city the crab fishers bring
their catch, solemnly bedded on ice, to the restaurants
where starred cooks with fast practiced hands
wreathe plates with dill and bay leaves as if for a
funeral or a poetry prize. I am told that
if you sit by the water in the old harbour
with the seafarers and exiles from Genoa, Venice,
Phoenicia, a sea otter might pay you a visit,
sleek robber, native of distant kelp forests,
slowly padding up the stone steps out of the estuary's
black stinking sludge, his inquisitive
demi-god's face turning to peer in puzzlement
at the alien upper world, where all is air
and movements have little weight, looking as if
he had stepped out of some aquatic fairy tale,
the water rolling off his grey pelt
in silvered drops, his whiskers abristle in the moonlight.
If the moon nets him out at sea in its trembling mesh
of beams it will release him with the other
species of misfits, those dreamers who drift in the water
with their hands folded and their eyes on the stars.
He will send them back into the dark depths.
He will move on to find other fish to snare.

Seeing Yellow

We brought sunflowers to the hospital, bought on impulse
on the street where lilies, hydrangeas, gerbera,
Chinese lanterns flared in pails and buckets, September's
extravaganza; but none
could rival the fire of the sunflowers – we held them
by their rough stalks like torches,
afraid of getting our fingers burnt.

Although the day was grey and wet, the streets
and buildings rain-darkened and cold, we walked
in a gorse spring light
all the way to the hospital,
our hands and faces bathed in yellow.
It had been mined at the core
of the earth, the pure, primary pigment
of ripe lemons or of van Gogh's wooden chair,
or borrowed from the angel in Padua, the one
we liked best, in the last row of the choir,
skinny, eyes kohl-rimmed, deep in the shadow
of a somber song, whose sketchy halo had slipped off
and clanked to the floor.

In the hospital, in crinkly plastic aprons and antiseptically washed,
we placed the sunflowers in his hands although we knew
he couldn't keep them – hospital rules – and saw
his face brighten. He was seated beside his bed as we approached,
all frailness in flannel robe and slippers,
in the discrete hush and clink of trollies wheeling past
with meal trays and water bottles, quietly reciting
a long-loved Catalan poem to himself and tapping its metre
on the arm of his chair with his fingers.
Sunflowers, he said, gladness and disbelief

in his voice, then after a pause, *I can see yellow.*
He put his hands around the flowers, he held them,
the round black faces inside their yellow ruffs.
Soleils noirs, he said, *Rimbaud
called them that,* and again with a laugh, *I can see yellow.*

We stood, looking at his fine, old man's face,
the rich white curls of his beard, his eyes humorous
behind thick lenses. We saw him at the edge
of a yellow field, the flowers swaying a little
on tall green stems around him,
their dark sun faces,
their yellow light.

My brother writes to me

Since April he's been counting swallows in the courtyard
from his own perch on the top floor. I know he is sleepless
with chemo, paces the rooms at night holding tête-à-têtes
eye-level with the moon in the skylight, waiting for morning.
He writes, the sky is smooth like a freshly ironed sheet,
a boundless playground ready for bold air surfers winging it up
    there, he is tense
with expectation. His ears are out for their tell-tale
shrill exuberant calls, his eyes on the look-out for their swift
    calligraphy,
faster than the fastest Chinese master's ink pen on a light blue page.
But there are fewer every year, he says, his census
of chimney swallows, house martins, swifts is dwindling – Frieder,
will we soon go around, heads down, afraid to look up
and find nothing there, no summer sky songs,
no speedy black nibs streaking the air.

II

My brother writes to tell me that starlings, those street-smart
    survivors,
are disappearing and that sparrows, crumb-stealing sans-culottes
of coffee tables, are threatened, too, not to speak of swallows
or swifts. I write back to describe our stroll on Fishermen's Island
in the middle of the city between high rises, where we recently heard
three nightingales sing in bright daylight; they come annually
to their breeding grounds on the island in a loop of the river
where the gardeners leave trees and undergrowth untouched just
    for them –
hence the jungle of nettles, tall grass, burdock, wild roses,
    pokeweed and tansy.

I tell him how one bird sat in a ragged weeping willow,
the other two somewhere aloft on a beech or chestnut, and how,
as seasoned spellbinders, they launched into a triple concerto
for fife, piccolo and penny whistle – three unseen musicians
    extemporizing,
and how we felt moved and softened yet never knew whence or
    why.

III

Speaking of starlings, remember that day in late summer –
the elderberries were ripe and the dark red umbels
hung low from the branches heavy with fruit, when the garden
suddenly filled with noise and a chattering flock of brown-
speckled birds wheeled down in one tattered cloud and spread
out over the elder tree by the back wall, wing-beating
and feeding in flight-mode at great speed.
This tree had caused me grief for years, I'd pruned away fungus
and dead wood, cut down the ivy, propped up sagging boughs,
freed leaves and flowers of black aphids, and in thanks it produced
frothy white blossoms each spring and in autumn
a rich harvest of berries, Remember I called you out onto the lawn.
Look, how the tree has grown wings, you said in surprise and delight.
Just look, the elder tree is taking flight.

IV

I tell my brother about the time I watched birds
through my camera's zoom as close as I could get to them –
it was on a busy city street in late spring. They were swallows
toing and froing at the top of an office block, twelve,
fifteen storeys high, feeding their young in nests glued to the ledges
of faux marble abutments – ancient adobe techniques

meeting slick twentieth-century glass, concrete and steel;
the parents were para-gliding down to the feeding grounds
of the canals and returning laden with catch,
and the fledglings I imagined I saw peeping over the ledge
open-beaked and hungry and secure in their cliff-face pueblo
above the city where the clouds cruised by very close
and the odd constellation drew near for a look at night: a dove,
a crow, a swan and a peacock, and occasionally, a bird of paradise.

V

Returning to nightingales, my brother and I agree it's a toss up
between their song and the blackbird's, but our hearts are moved
    more
by the balladeer of chimney tops, his nimble variations on door bells,
sirens, dog whistles grafted into the sweet stanzas he sings at sunrise,
impatient for the whole world to wake up and hear. One spring,
    my brother says,
he was followed around Europe from East to West by the same
    blackbird's
melodies outside his window each night. I tell him there's a nest
    safely tucked
into an ivy-screened fork of the elder tree, guarded by the birds'
warning calls and yellow-ringed eyes. The neighbourhood cats
tread warily around him, for they know to beware of his anger.
And in winter, I say, we leave apples for the blackbirds in the
    garden, cut in half.
They scoop out the flesh and in return we find the skins
in the grass with the core left intact, heart-shaped, deftly sculpted.
Amsel, hermit's companion, amsala, merula, merel, merle noir.

VI

The latest reports from my brother are hopeful. He is in remission,
    released
from the bleak room where he used to sit, his hands up to their wrists
in crushed ice, listening to Chopin on his earphones while the
    mixture dripped
into his vein. The cell count's down to normal after months of
    this, secondaries
stilled or gone. I tell him about my discovery at a busy junction
    where
on a traffic island near the Turkish Market someone has planted
a garden, one of many that have cropped up around the city,
unexpected amidst the oceanic roar of motors. This one's been let
    run wild,
all greens and yellows, goldenrods, evening primrose and above all
dozens of sunflowers, teeming with insects and sparrows who gather
to feast on seeds in the densely packed flower heads, many of
    them adroop
with their own weight, the coarse stalks listing or bent over. Frieder,
let's celebrate in the rough garden with the riffraff of city streets
    who don't sow
or reap. Let's offer up a libation in thanks and to appease the
    jealous fates.

Lament for the Birds

for Benji

I

The passenger pigeon, the Carolina parakeet, the veery,
the Labrador duck, the great auk, the scarlet tanager –

and many many more, all the countless
others, the thousands I shot with fine shot,

the ivory-billed woodpecker, the painted bunting,
the red-cockaded warbler, the harlequin duck –

bound and trussed, skewered and wired
to make them look more natural than nature
could ever make them look,

the peregrine falcon, the redhead, the lazuli finch,
the black-and-white warbler, the red-eyed vireo –

that was the art – true to life, life-size, caught in flight
or mid-hunt or picking fruit of a shrub,

the Arkansas siskin, the ruby-crowned kinglet,
the American flamingo, Bachmann's warbler –

nesting, dreaming on a flowering branch
or singing their sweet hearts out
or uttering raucous triumphant squawks,

the great white egret, the Carolina titmouse,
the wood thrush, the mocking bird –

sounding a shrill warble or as if they were shaking a rattle
or calling me into the wilderness,

the Esquimaux curlew, the green-winged teal,
the foolish guillemot, the great loon above all –

with its seductive melancholy call
that might lure one out onto the misty Great Lake,

I wish I could give them all back to the air,
all those thousands I killed and portrayed:

Fearlessly he awaited my approach,
looking upon me with undaunted eye. I fired and he fell...

the prairie starling, the ruby-throated hummingbird,
the green-winged teal, the great cinereous owl –

True to life, four hundred and thirty-five life-sized
watercolours of birds, stopped mid-movement,
voiceless, dead as dodos.

II

Always I am portrayed with a rifle
instead of a pen or brush, yes, some days I shot hundreds.
My life spanned two continents, I escaped
from revolutionary France to revolutionary America
where I was able to indulge my passion.

I became a good artist, I think. Less skilful
at business I lost more than one fortune
and so I became a part of the many at the frontier
pushing West, I took on the colouring

of a frontier's man: the long hair, narrowed eyes
always looking into the far distance,
the long stride of the wilderness dweller.

III

Art conceals the wounds where the bullets entered
or the grape shot.
The exquisite charm of my watercolours
covered them over with a sheen that hardened
like champlevé enamel.

Study, specimen, taxonomy, classification,
the instruments: pins, nails, hammers, wire
secateurs and always the gun.

There was so much death I had to be quick
to create beauty out of decay, always aware
of the contrast between the iridescent plumage
and the parasites at work already eating into the flesh.

What is the two-dimensional image
compared to the warm body with breathing lungs,
a throat giving voice to sweet or harsh sounds,
to mating calls or danger alarms?

I felt an intimacy with them bordering on frenzy.

I knew them, their frolics, and fights,
their feeding habits, their habitats, and how they cared
for their nestlings. I observed them
as they took to the air or rested on a slow-meandering water,
sang at dawn, soared above the endless prairies
or fell like stars from the sky into the river
to catch their prey.

I saw Carolina parakeets gathered in the centre of a grain field
like *a brilliantly coloured carpet,*
I saw brown pelicans fishing the shallows
of the Ohio river and bald eagles nesting by the hundreds
along the Mississippi. I kept notes at all times:

The air was literally filled with pigeons ...

the passing flock turned the day to night, they were so plentiful,
pink-breasted passenger pigeons, now gone,
vanished from the air.

What happened is well-known, I turned my passion,
my calling, into my trade, a great mistake, something
that takes on a deadly momentum of its own.
We see it every day around us – the pursuit
of profit doesn't spare lives, it stops for nothing and no one.

Before it's too late and you are left with no more
than vast killing fields, silent forests, empty skies,
I ask you: Give them back to the air
while it is still in your power to do so.
I ask of you, give them back.

Near Gare de l'Est

Ohne Musik wäre das Leben ein Irrtum.
  —Friedrich Nietzsche

All evening you search for music, you walk the long river
in a wind tunnel of engine noise and petrol fumes
and when you arrive pigeons mock you from the top
of the barred concert hall. A moustachioed angel waves you aside.
Later, in a nameless café near Gare de l'Est, there is Mozart
on the CD player, the *Piano Concerto in A*. The spirit of music
has come to you across the city in the guise of a young man in jeans
who works behind the bar, shaven-headed, two studs in his left brow,
his T-shirt announcing TALK IS CHEAP. He hums along as he goes
around stacking chairs, wiping a table top and, after the last
movement's cadenza has gathered to its final back-lit cascade,
he changes the CD to Bach – the *Well-Tempered Clavier*
played by Glenn Gould. No one speaks, there's no sound
among the lustre of brass and espresso machines except Bach,
just slight clinks of glass, an occasional jangle of stainless steel
and a distant percussive rumble or is it the city
pressing its ear to the windows to listen? A salesman near you
with his case of samples, a woman who's been staring at her Mac,
and in the shadows further back more people sit with their eyes
    closed.
As the ship rises from a nocturnal sea, prow and railings looped
with lights, you know there is room for all on its splendid decks,
serene progressions that overcome any barrier in the October night.
In the station trains pull to a stop, hundreds assemble and disperse
    again
like black-clad choruses who still have far to go. With flashing
    signals,
planes sail into the sky above Paris and on the junctions
traffic conductors turn and dance taking their bows. The music flows

under the city's bridges lighting up the nooks
where the sorrowful and lost wait. It says, *take up your bed and walk*
It says, *come, the tables are prepared.* As Glenn Gould's fingers
spell it out on the piano keys, note by pure note,
he groans now and then with the great strains of his task.

The Irish Tenor Michael Kelly Recalls Mozart in Paris

I will never forget him wrapped in his greatcoat
against the icy blasts as he strode past the liveried
hauteur of tall gates, first citizen of the Republic
of music, a small figure, nondescript,
with bulging eyes, as the poet Tieck depicted
him, or picking his way through stench and dirt
of Paris streets, an immigré rehearsing the words
for coldness of heart in the local argot.
They kept him waiting for hours
in freezing ante-rooms, in arctic salons
while his fingers turned numb, gave him out of tune
clavichords, the lords and ladies turning deaf ears,
when he played only the armchairs
and walls listened. Years before, Paris had begun with
so much promise. Fingers on the keyboard, his,
his sister's, Piano Sonata for four hands. Divine,
they applauded, a mere child, C-Major, the key
of light. To this day I see him hurry
through the dark winter streets, snow
powdering his wig, shoulders, through muddy lanes,
past candelabra flickering in tall windows,
his mother dying in the hotel. *Prego,
di pardonarmi, carissima,* he wrote. (The irony
of today's plaque: *Mozart et sa mère Maria séjournèrent ici.*)
He did all he could but *failed to please.*
No, he was not a great success,
the Parisian Symphony, fireworks and fanfares
for Legros and stupid donkeys that lacked ears.
*Dear father, I could do nothing in this place
of coldness,* he wrote to Leopold. Always he fell

short, always he apologized. Paris
was a flop, his name at the end of a long playbill.
But whenever I sang Tamino's aria *'Dies Bildnis
ist bezaubernd schön ...'* it was inexplicable,
and – forgive the cliché – unearthly, a work of genius.
What its mystery is, who can tell?
Perhaps this music's naked appeal
to the heart. Yes, he talked of an emptiness that pains.
Destitute, he was still able to be pleased
that his dear 'Papa Haydn' was fêted in England.
And in the end? He was drained,
sick of playing the clown –
his *canto funèbre?* He had to leave it undone.

Riddle Canon

for Leo Treitler

On his 1746 Leipzig portrait Bach playfully
held the sheet with the music
upside down –

***

he turned it by 180 degrees –
a page spiralled to the ground,
a page spiralled upwards

***

the echo of a canon, a fugue, a flight
beneath the longhaired willows
that were as bespangled in the spring sun
as the king with his Machiavelli eyes
and silver flute

***

as if Bach were running in his Leipzig boots
across the cobbled square, his footsteps
pursued by the echo of footsteps
running twice as fast
in the opposite direction

***

the trick was to let the notes wander
like ants on the edge

of a Moebius strip
travelling along and exchanging sides
without collision in a continuous
circular motion

***

like Ouroborus, the serpent
who symbolizes the soul of the world
the beginning and end of time
eating its own tail

***

the royal theme reappeared –
a six-voice fugue *ricercar* –
'in contrary motion'
in the crab canon,
then upside down and then
in a mirrored upside down crab canon
and so forth

***

music turned on its head
as in the Leipzig portrait –
reflected in a glass ball
rolling

Berlin Diary

Görlitzer Park (January)

Soccer playing fields
white in the glare of floodlights.
Flags rolled up and stiff.

Bethaniendamm (February)

Where the wall once curved
round the church of St. Thomas
an orbiting car.

Landwehrkanal (March)

Swans drift one way, boats
another, water pulls the
ground from under me.

U-1 Schlesisches Tor (April)

Buy the *Homeless News*
from Schemkel, nervous angel
with his frayed halo.

Lohmühle (May)

Round the trailer park
mongrels sleep on cobbles.
The smell of diesel.

Prinzessinengarten (June)

Poppy-coloured head-
scarves in a circle among
vegetables and flowers.

Kottbusser Tor (July)

Girl with blue hair and
eight colour spray-cans: one
more than the rainbow.

Görlitzerstrasse (August)

In late summer. wheat
and rye grow through the pavements,
the sparrow's pickings.

Mariannenplatz (September)

Neighbourhood party.
For mild-mannered Dobermans
a land of cockaign.

Falckensteinstrasse (October)

Democratic streets.
Pumpkins and trumpet solos
of a Roma band.

Lübbenerstrasse (November)

Where three women sat –
a carpet of nutshells in
the light of gas lamps.

Oberbaumbrücke (December)

In the red-brick vaults
of the bridge a busker plays
ice crystal music.

Forefathers

Little about them is known to me,
those three ghostly figures on a fading photograph:
my great-grandfather and his brothers,

(one a composer of hymns), white-bearded
patriarchs, seated around a table;
the insignia of pastoral office: frock coats

buttoned up to their necks, white collars,
almost like Dutch burghers
from the Golden Age. Their expressions are stern

yet mild. But what about the pain
behind their temples where a vein throbbed
against doubt, or the daily drudge:

the drone of the parlour organ
and the congregation's thin tremolo,
the smell of soup ladled to the poor

or the books in Hebrew, Greek or Latin
studied till late and questioned
by the light of paraffin lamps,

the preludes and fugues practiced for hours
ad gloriam dei. Did they choose it freely?
the self-denial, the desperate clinging

to vague reports of some outlandish miracle
of long ago? In the lanes
near their parsonages the carnival

of roses, the revelry of summer, the stink
of manure, of slaughter, blood and rebirth,
sharp as a sudden arousal.

The farmers worshipped other gods
in the pub or their marriage beds,
and on feast days brought their offerings:

sugared doughnuts, sausages,
blood puddings, the unloved
viscera of their animals.

If I met my forefathers today
would they try to gather me up –
clearly a lost sheep – to return me

to a flock that has long dispersed?
Or would they touch my head
in bewilderment and blessing?

Heimat

Small, non-descript streets – the houses crouched, fearful
as first graders in grey rows – named after forgotten poets
whose patriotic songs were hollow as organ pipes.

The streets had escaped the war. History had passed them over,
impatient for more momentous locations,
greater glories and catastrophes. The shadows of cruelty

and shame lifted gradually, brooms swept the ashes
from the footpaths, forgetting grew like hair or fingernails
and now the houses were mostly busy

with radishes and gooseberries in the gardens and lilacs
that hung over the fences, with washing lines, lace curtains,
the evening news and the punctual smell of cooking.

Among the streets there was one with aspirations: it had a church
at one end, a pub at the other and in the middle a grocery shop
entitled Colonial Wares. The grocer's wife had angry eyes

and ladled out oat flakes and flour from wooden drawers
where meal worms lived pale untroubled lives. In the evenings
the older boys in the houses were sent to the pub

and returned carrying frothing beer mugs home
to their sullen-faced fathers, back from shift work,
who hated the noise of children at play.

They'd sit alone in the rooms, bent
over their butterfly collections, or the pre-war
fighter plane series on twenty pfennig stamps.

The bell, the slow iron heart of the tall clock tower,
beat out each quarter hour and a sleepy cloud
floated past to rest on the red saddle roof of the church.

At first light on May mornings processions passed
along the street to the church, the murmured prayers
rustling like starched white communion dresses.

The whispering of many voices woke the spiders in the gardens
and, stiff-legged, they climbed the lilac trees to hang up
their geometrical masterpieces.

The blackbirds varied their morning stanzas
with dog whistles, and the church doors
slowly swallowed up the processions.

Inside, the sacrificial red heart wreathed with thorns
lay on a high winged altar, the community ate the body,
the priest tasted the blood.

Although I often dreamed it as a child,
the church never burst into flames nor did
the tower collapse and bury our house beneath it

and its cannon-heavy bell. The cloud, however,
has slipped off the roof of the church long ago
and the sun hides behind it and it feels cold.

By the River

The name is derived from Latin virda *meaning strong, fast, green.*

1.
Since I could not step into the same river twice
    I stepped into the name —*Wertach,*
    ankle-deep in cold fire,
        a green ice-
sheet splintering on the low weirs –

adrift with liquid cloud shadow,
    pools beneath willows
    glinting, trout-streaked,
rough water from glacial peaks.

2.

In school we learned
    how a trickle of ice melt in the mountains
grew into a fast winding stream,
    flowed along a glacier-carved plain

    to a confluence where Roman legions
set up camp, stabled their horses
        and angled for pike and char,

how the blood of many, of heretics and martyrs,
    Jews, witches, soldiers,
    ran as a dark undercurrent through its long story

and how over the millennia a city arose
    with curving bridges, fountains and spires,

        the turning wheels
of factories, fairgrounds and windmills.

3.

I went back, crossed the wooden foot bridge –
        its roof shingled as the cone of an Iceland pine –

and looked down where the grey river
        unravelled in the power station, a red-

brick monument to a modernism now dead.

Turbines churned up the water
        spume rose like smoke – an offering

to steel age gods – then it emerged beyond the weir,
        glistening, victorious.

4.

I might have gone past without seeing
but the river raised green shutters
on the wilderness by its banks;

it prattled with pebbles
and water spiders,
welcomed me to meadows

of sweet grasses,
ground elder and yarrow,
blue bugle weed, cuckoo flower.

Beetles like miniature knights
chiselled from jet were dispatched
on impossible errands

and a congregation of snails
was put in charge of the long afternoon's
time management.

5.

The footpath lost itself
in a green tangle,
a childhood riddle
of brambles and nettles
but the child's memories course
through the blood
and the pebble still tastes
of ice and heat.

Fashions

Sometimes the garden gates of memory swing open
and the women of my childhood street pass through,
arm in arm with long steps and the padded shoulders
and tight belts of past fashion. It was
the era of swing, of bakelite telephones,
kidney tables, kiss-proof lipsticks.

The women coiled their hair into chignons talking
with mouths full of hairpins. Their taciturn husbands
had come back from the war minus an eye or a limb
but never spoke about it, though sometimes they beat
one of the children for no reason. In the mornings
the women fastened their husband's empty shirtsleeves
or trouser legs neatly like envelopes
containing angry messages.

The symbols had been prised from public buildings
leaving ugly stains, and street signs lay
in the half-lit bottom of the river bed
among badges and medals. This was the new time,
the past had been folded and stored away,
the rubble cleared –
new buildings rose, new styles.

They kept up with trends, the neighbours
from my almost forgotten childhood,
with their Eau de Colognes, pencil skirts,
and practical sewing tips.

Which goddess of chic and common sense
held her hands over them? Over cotton frocks
printed with daisy motifs, over coral necklaces

whose beads were deeper red than blood,
the lace collars like two half-moons
resting on pale or freckled collar bones,
the hourglass waists, the bowed heads
with the straight parting and the kiss curl
and, above all, over the watchful eyes
beneath pillbox hats trimmed with veils
in which tiny enamelled beetles were trapped.

Paternoster

I

Strictly out of bounds, it rose
up from the marble lobby, silent, grandiose,
rose past me towards the top floors,

and I, eleven years old in my winter coat,
and with no business in the civic offices, stood,
twofold transgressor – trespasser

and, what was worse, truant from school –
stood lost, free and emboldened,
waiting to jump into a cubicle and ascend

towards the mystery of floor ten or twelve, sole
passenger, and knowing it was now
or never still I stood, faltering,

while it passed unstoppably down into cellar darkness,
the winter day already turning into night, sank down
into the land of shades below

only to reappear again to me this minute:
ghost chariot rising from lost years

lifting me with my school bag filled
with little learning, many joyless hours.

II

When our Latin teacher entered
slamming the door, we froze,
paper planes stopped mid-air,
the windows frosted up. We rose
to say: *Pater noster
qui es in caelis, sanctificetur
nomen tuum* ... in a half whisper
terrified of the teacher's wrath;
then it was the passive voice,
the o-declination,
the *veni vidi vici* of conquest;

and in my day-dreams I saw it then
passing through the sunlit sky-light windows
of the tax office,
and no promise
et dimmitte nobis ...
of forgiveness
for my trespasses
in sight.

III

We don't know it anymore, the *perpetuum mobile*
of teak-panelled cubicles,
rising past executive floors, stairwells,

tea kitchens, offices, broom closets.
There was only one right moment to step in,
a second's doubt would leave you standing

and while you still faltered
people appeared and vanished on their way
like ghosts, heads or feet first or last,

buckle pumps, slip-ons, trousers
with sharp creases, legs in sheer hosiery,
rose or descended,

polyester shirts, spotless white blouses,
earnest frowning faces,
glided up or down,

secretaries with butterfly glasses,
permanent frizzes, lipstick,
acne and duck tails on apprentice clerks,

now swept away together with polished brass, teak
paneling, card indexes, dial phones,
endless afternoons, all gone

through the shredder, unstoppable
as the paternoster, oh, but
the second of taking the leap –

tired and heavy souls
stepping one by one from dark cages
into the open evening.

J. E. Hall of Dartford, first installed the Cyclic Elevator in the Oriel Chambers of Liverpool in England in 1884

Small Railway Stations

As far as they were concerned, Ionic porticoes
had not been invented, pillars or rosette
windows, marble, mosaic – they left all this circus
to the important stations in the cities
with their tracks to far-flung places
where passengers sat in the waiting rooms,
their eyes on the hands of the huge brass clock –

no, the small stations were low, built of blackened brick,
a box of pansies their sole embellishment
on the sill where the cat slept.
Inside, the windows were the undisputed domain
of the common house fly. News from nebulous distances
ticked on the telegraphs; the tapes grew and curled unread
till they reached the floor. Poppies flourished between the tracks
and if you put your ear to a mast
you could hear an insect hum at its core.
The stationmaster's red cap glowed in the sun
like a warning signal. Never did the express to the capital
stop here but carriages of local trains
followed the slow curve down the valley
behind an engine that steamed and whistled in protest.

It's years since the small stations were erased from the maps
and closed down. They are pizzerias now, sports bars,
youth clubs; nothing happens here, no more departures,
tears, welcoming embraces. But once I found myself
in a café in one of those forgotten stations
and on the platform saw the place name: Langendreer –
this was the station where my mother had left
for her studies in a remote city.

She must have stood here waiting for the train
in her burgundy coat and black velvet hat,
a serious young girl with a small cardboard valise beside her.
She was spirited from here to other stations, more momentous
than this one, she was blown farther
and farther away into the disasters and joys
of her time, its terrors and solemn moments,
with nothing but her light luggage.

Song

for Adrian, Cliodhna, Clea and Lesy

The children played in a narrow back garden
without end. Behind its rough stone wall
the town began, full of its own importance,
covering a small part of the earth

with solemn buildings, canals and streets.
Seagulls stood watch above the garden
balanced on thermals, and a septet
of sharp-eyed geese passed overhead

in a music of strong white wings.
The green boat of the garden had long
grown roots into the ground and lay
dreaming of ocean forests, of ferrying

the children through blue fields of water.
At times the days were short. Then the windows
in the house peered out into the rain
full of a curious orange glow,

but on June nights the elder trees lit their dim lanterns
and the blackbird sang until late its sweet
unending variations. They played with twigs,
snails, a blue-veined stone.

The twigs promised a star, the snails
promised a journey, the stone promised
a half moon, a circus tent, a handful of red
berries, a water mill, a nest with five nestlings,

an apple tree beneath which a pair
of small capable watch dogs were asleep,
a new sister, a book whose covers
were green as the boat in the grass, green

as the windfall apples, the poplars beyond
the canal. As the evening light faded
we watched them rewrite on its pages
the chapters of our beginnings in a script we had lost.

A bird raised its piccolo to play a tune,
a cloud looked down and sailed past.

Brooklyn Morning Weddings

The morning was innocent, it was a young child still
rolling its blue dice across the roof tops of the city
and through its dark canyons, not caring
what would become of the day,

And nothing could have been more guileless
than the sun rising on the East River – its banks
still in darkness – turning the waltzing beat of Manhattan
into an atonal composer's glittering soundscape.

We crossed the river in a rattling carriage.
Three black buskers performed for us,
juggled and swung off the handrails defying gravity
in all their young muscular grace and thoughtlessness,

That day with a light-hearted wind off distant forests
and small boats abob on waves near Pier Five
with their old ladies' names, *Agnes, Clarissa, Griseldis*,
penciled in with pastel colours,

we walked into the shadow below Brooklyn Bridge,
and nothing could have been more surprising
than the warm smell of cinnamon and honey welcoming us,
the fires and the white golden dough baking

in preparation for banquets.
And then we saw them arriving: the white,
the orange, purple and blue wedding parties,
brides and bridesmaids in dresses more scalloped and sheer

than rare, tropical blossoms,
and the boys, taking their colours from them,

wore matching suits and ties; it seemed the rainbow
ended here on the river banks below the bridge.

Whatever hardship had brought them to the benevolent,
air-bridged harbour from distant worlds, that day
of the weddings they came from all boroughs of the city,
from Queens, the Bronx, Brooklyn, Staten Island, Manhattan,

migrating in their dozens with gifts of rosemary
and myrtle for the goddess; entire flocks of families,
best men, parents, children and friends,
with the couples islanded amidst them

and the city open wide to them all.
Let the small crafts take off for Cythera with a cargo
of worshippers, trailing a droplet-embroidered
wake behind them.

Let dozens of volleyballs nearby in the courts fly heavenwards
in ecstasy, let the brides step into the arms
of their grooms at the instant the quick-winged light
touches the crowns of their heads.

First Snow

Years ago when we moved in we looked down
on the apple tree in the backyard
below our first floor balcony.

Never pruned, it shot up tall and slim
as no apple tree ever should, reaching
for the light, higher
than our windows by now,

I wonder does it fancy itself as a poplar,
head and shoulders
above the wild cherry and plum trees around it.

At night during summer
the leaves flickered black against the glare
of the backdoor lights,

but they are all gone now
and overnight someone
has daubed the garden with white chalk

and blown a fine white dust
on the bare branches
that are still hung with a few yellow

December apples, sweet offerings
for sparrows, for lost migrant birds.

Oliphant Palace

The ton weight of her rump sways
to an inner rhythm, a music only she obeys
that keeps her rocking leisurely

on her legs, those colossal wrink-
led columns, rough as tree bark,
her trunk swinging in wide arcs

as she stands in the quad of the faux-Mogul
palace where all except her are scaled-
down, and in the side aisles

the colourful cats are curled up asleep
in a niche, or circle, or lope
across gypsum rocks. Old matriarch, she gropes

and fingers strands of hay and feeds
her daughters with delicate
precision, mindful of sparrows between her feet,

and what a fanfare when she raises her trunk to the sky,
lets rip a trumpet call from savannah days
hailing the zookeeper who is busy

shovelling golden dung into creels.
She hardly looks at me but I can feel
a massive intelligence taking my measure coolly

as the grey-lashed eye pans
across us, a row of indistinct faces beyond
the compound wall, and is lowered again,

neither judges nor reveals, aloof as a queen
alone on a sun-struck arid plain:
the memories, the glamour, the pain.

Still Lifes

Five raisins held tight
in the fist of the woman
found dead in her flat.

The cathedral is
standing in the rain, the bells
are hoarse from the cold.

The clock stopped working.
Twice daily it warns me that
it is two to twelve.

A hare, a tumbler
with a tear drop from Brabant.
Who left in a rush?

Cows graze, throwing long
shadows on green fields, tiny
in the hawk's eye.

Snow falls on the bronze
pianist's hands playing the air
of silent falling.

Wilderness

No matter how elegant the cut of our clothes may be,
we remain creatures of the wild and should never forget that.
    —Charles Forster

Not a childhood dream, more a destiny –
my other life as badger, otter, fox,
after I went down on all fours, a woodland demon, calloused
as Caliban, I crept from my den, earth-matted, snarling,
snuffling, to forage across the forest floor, springy
as a sponge with decay and moss; I loved its cold pliant effluvium.
Under cover of broad-leafs, my face buried in roots,
I abandoned the tyranny of sight, deep in the obscurity
of rotting wood and skunk cabbage, I learned fast
that eyes were useless in the undergrowth.
There was a time I'd have stopped to admire
the minuscule green stars of sphagnum, the blown-glass
flutes of the white cap or the dark brown stag beetle's
polished wing case, but not now, not since I'd learned
a new language of odours: the sly silken aroma
of the deadly angel mushroom, the stinkhorn's
carrion reek, the multiple fragrances of humus,
tree bark, animal droppings, my own excretions,
the fabled scent of spring, its honeyed dust
that lined the small streams. My ears, sharpened
by night and fear, became attuned
to the birds' warning calls, I knew the portent
of each crackle and rustle, the snap
of twigs underfoot, wolf tread
and the slim percussive trot of deer, the slightest change
in the tinnitus pitch of the insects,
and above all the echoing sun-streaked silences
among the tall trunks, imposing

as an unplayed cathedral organ.
The kindness of the wild embraced me
with all its smells, sounds and tastes, I lay
on its prayer rug, on blue anemones interwoven
with nettle, bull thistle and devil's club; nothing
in my diet repelled me, not the grey-white texture of grubs,
or the slippery salt-foam of slugs, my tongue
was taught a new vernacular of tang and relish,
rodent blood, the sweet crunch of lichens and fungi,
I traded language in for another form
of utterance, and quickly
the images conjured up by words faded, no concept
came between me and oak, whitebeam
hazel bush or the deadly nightshade,
not even the delicacy of the stardust web,
the wire-brush tufts of grey wolf lichen, the detail
and structural accuracy of the beechnut,
the smoky odour of tree sap where lightning
had struck, I inhaled it deeply stalking my prey
thoughtless, without compassion.

Now that I am back among beds, laptops
and coffee cups, I try to adjust to straight-backed
chairs and plush sofas, to relearn the use
of clothing, of doors, stairs, knives and guns,
but whenever I bend over to kiss a man's face
I catch the smell issuing from beneath aftershave,
epidermis, subcutis, from the closed loop
of the moving blood, from the core of life itself,
the perfume of unstoppable decay, its rank
simmering froth, its spectral iridescence.
I had been tutored well by my feral instructors,
my fellow creatures of the wilderness,
oh life, inseparable from death,
beautiful intoxication, dogged, bizarre.

Zoo

penguin

black bottle
with white label
put on ice
for undertaker funerals.

porcupine

the forest's pincushion
it hates being needled

tortoise

of the fourth dimension
it crawls
from slow space to curved time

cormorant

the cormorant on the rocks
out beyond the docks
shakes his wing
the crazy thing
not politely but contritely

armadillo

between the avocado bushes
chain-mail
by special delivery

old bear

on the freeway
her coat dusty and threadbare
like an old sofa

she has come inland
to search for the bees
of the horizon

Nocturama

*And when night comes I'll go
to places fit for woe.*
　　—William Blake

Unseeing I went underground,
followed the arrow into night-
desert, night-scree, night-burrow.
What was it that touched my cheek, a finger,
a snout, a wing, some softly breathing memory?
What was it that fluttered in my head,
what bird perched in my heart pressing it
against my ribs? And everywhere eyes
that saw where I saw nothing, irises
huge and polished as magnifying glasses,
the obsidian dots of pupils at the centre
pooling the night. Guarded by
the sleepy-eyed owl, my sisters civet
and lori, I grew incisors and talons,
my eyes were hooded, I was guided
by scent, my voice broke,
I lived in league with the aardvark.

Lives

for Miriam

Remember the women on Chignac market?
How beautiful they were, how they weighed our
purchases with their strong hands, artichokes
with overlapping Saurian green leaves,

at the centre a tender heart in its nest of spikes
a harpy would have for dessert,
or onions in sheer skins, brown as pantyhose
that, cut in half, would bring quick tears to your eyes?

How the women would scoop from rustling
hessian sacks walnuts that looked
like tiny shrunken brains
to which blackened skin still stuck,

how a dark red fluid oozed from
their fruit and vegetable crates,
and how they would scrutinize us with hard
blue eyes that had narrowed from squinting

at the sun in gardens and vineyards,
at their kitchens, the floor tiles and knives,
at the glaring neglect by their husbands,
the blinding failures of their children.

Daily they dieted on rage and sent us packing
with our loads and wishes back
to our lives in grey countries with long shadows –
or so they must have looked to them

from the other side of their silver scales.
How we wanted to be them, how we wanted to say:
how can I be of help, monsieur, these red
cherries are so very sweet; madame,

take one, taste this plum, its skin
is swollen with juice, take it between
your teeth and bite, it is delicious. Trust me,
I know, see my lips, my purple tongue.

Summer with Juan Miró

Not *Vegetable Garden with Donkey* but
a garden the Pythia might have had
away from oracles, this orchard of orange trees

and dry, prickly grass where daily an old woman
shawled in black brought her chestnut stallion to feed
on the windfall oranges – we saw

his russet coat flash through the cross-
hatchings of light and shade. At night
she returned to fetch him, never replied

to calls or greetings, *a prophetess,*
we joked, *with handfuls of black and white beans
in her pocket.* We lived through that summer of heat,

downpours, lightning and thunder, careless,
in a ramshackle hayshed with erratic roof
tiling. When the wind rose before a storm and moved the trees,

the air filled with citrus smells and we closed
our eyes and saw Miró paintings of our own:
bird and insect constellations, cyphers

and star signs, the nocturnal centipedes
with which we shared the bare floorboards
of our room, black before orange.

In the evenings young men and women
came from the village to eat with us,
drink resinous wine and sing popular songs:
the general's son, the spy, the lame-

footed dissident we nicknamed Oedipus,
Aliki, the goddess look-alike with flashing eyes.

And nightly before sunrise we heard it, a panting
and rustling in the dark garden, a hurried
unnameable activity, dry twigs snapping underfoot,

sounds of tearing, crackling, hissing, a growl, a throttled cry.
It was as though a ghostly militia were passing
through the garden, set on pillage and murder.

We never knew was it animal or human
and never rose to watch but every morning found
the relics of a feast or sacrifice strewn about,

gnawed bread, bones, shreds of paper, blood,
or was it the red wine bottle turned over? After we left
we went our different ways, never talked

of the garden again. We were too afraid all our lives
to ask what the answer would have been for us:
white for yes, black for no.

Jesus in Mayo

Too far distant to be sure as the bus lurches
and slows at the T-junction in the driving rain
whether the whitish figure hanging between
the trees at the back of the playing field
is the fleeting after-image of some murderous après-midi
sacrifice, some rushed, hushed-up afternoon
mob's blood-sports near the god-forsaken
hard shoulder where drizzle-slickened country-
roads join in a cross of sorts and no man
in his right mind would intervene nor kneel
before his open-armed Do Not Pass appeal,
bestowing blessings of smudged ashes
and rain on penitent foreheads, a roadside
saviour, resin and gypsum, bemired and moss-
streaked and what's more barely held together by
rusted chicken-wire and plaster of Paris bandages.
I ask you, Jesus in Mayo-God-help-us, have mercy
and bless us for better or worse, turn
towards us and bless this evening that's washed out
on bus shelter roofs and tarmac in small town
squares, bless the Thai Orchard Take Away
the Golden Seas chipper, the Coffee-to-Go café,
the Last Reductions Emporium, the billboard
commanding *Walk the Walk*, the Swallow's Nest
Public House and the Eye Candy Properties, not least
their proprietor Mr. Louis T. Lynx and the man on his ladder
in white overalls who's fixing a street-
lamp, the empty boom-time villas, the White Cow water
tower and the hooded crows that scatter
from the tower like wet grape shot, bless villages, hills,
hedgerows and farms with their steaming barns
the T-Junction and the sodden playing fields,

bless plaster, paint and resin, the poor and raw materials of our adoration, frankincense, blood and bitumen.

Sister Hildegard at 98 Considers Her Life

As a girl all I wanted was to be a parachutist
like Lilly Byczkowsky, my heroine –
a tiny figure in the centre of a silken bell, airlifted
into the high blue theatre of the sky –
or a pilot, a flight traffic controller, anything
to do with the heavens. I wanted to know

what was going on there. I still do. Nightly
I stand by the window of my cell – girded
and ready in my black tunic, cingulum, white veil, black veil –
and watch the planes, those metallic science-fiction angels,
circle above Frankfurt airport, hear them
growl evangels at the lit-up city below.

You agnostics sadden me, how will you ever
grasp what happened? I was young, fiery, the tapestries
were spread out before me with their streams and
forests of wild beasts. Why did I not enter them?
A voice called, come, what could I do? I said, Jesus, surely
not me, not now, not yet. But I went, just like that. I fell

without even a parachute to hold on to, I fell, taking
the thermals on trust. And what for? A niche in the cemetery wall?
Was it all worth it, the chilly vespers, more a cantata of coughs
than hosannas, winter mornings in the steamed-up convent laundry,
chilblains, years of fasting and obedience, the mysterious rustle of
    habit fabrics,
the whispered envious gossip, soot and alabaster in altarpieces,

baroque clouds and the eyes of the Saviour picked out with gold
leaf? I, too, saw blood seeping from embroideries and bell towers
    ablaze

with stigmata. But all this is long past.
Empty, scoured, almost transparent, light as parachute silk,
I am only the conduit through which blessings pass
from him to me to you and you — watch out, pass them on.

Trompe-l'Oeil

American, 1890

Look, inside the oak frame there's another second one –
lacquered cherry wood – and within the painting
another painting, an ornamental hearth
with banked fire, bellows, coal buckets, a realistic
pioneer interior, homely – American pastoral – and see
how everything's so still, you wish for some life,
maybe a cat asleep on the rug, a fly buzzing around the light
or that someone whose hands, ringed and scented
or rough from work, would stoke the glowing embers,
would rattle on the grate with a shovel; and see
above the mantel rifles, crossed rapiers and trophies –
the glass-eyed head of a fox, a wild ram's curled horns –
you have to admire the painter's skill, how he makes
your eye believe in the three dimensions
and how easily he fools it – the eye is slow to pick up
warning signs that say: nothing is as it seems here, look closely:
inside the shut room there's another room where someone
has turned the key on some calamity and walked away
from the spreading stain, from dead silence falling,
settling like soot on the mantelpiece, the jugs, the silver
candle sticks, even the storm lamps, dulling the varnish,
the gleaming surfaces. And observe the shadows
behind the shadows, (what masterly shading
of blacks!) and the yellowed note pinned to the wall,
the letters so precisely drawn you can almost read
the message, but not quite which is a mercy because
you won't know, should you be alarmed,
and why does the sight of the grey moth clinging
to a papery flower head, its wings of ashes and snow
stiffly folded, cause you such anguish you have to turn away?
Perhaps nobody loves us?

The China Shop Prepares for the Visit of the Elephant

Everyone assembled? Ming, Tang, Ding?
Kamakura, Raku? Sèvres, Wedgewood,
Nymphenburg? Limoges, Meissen,
Venice? Beleek, Royal Copenhagen?
Yes? Very good. Friends, we have all
been through the heat of the kilns,
we have been fired, hardened,
glazed, enameled, burnished
and encrusted. We are phoenixes
rising from the ashes, not neophytes.
As guardians of refinement and tradition
of beauty, elegance, form and function we are service-
able and a delight to the eye and the touch.
We are delicate but strong.
It's good to remember that in times of crisis.
Comrades, you all know the visit
of the elephant is impending again.
This time reports have reached us
that are even more than usually alarming
before this always nerve-racking event:
the elephant elected to the leadership
of the savannahs for this legislative period
is preceded by a reputation that is worrying
to say the least even among loxodonta: he is said
to be erratic, uncouth, deceitful, nasty,
cunning, vengeful, stupid and above all a bully.
He is lecherous and vain, although he is not
a pretty sight himself with his old
wrinkled trunk and his wispy tail.
He likes to hang out with other bullies
hardcore proboscidean supremacists,

experts at muck-raking, smear campaigns,
trampling the grass roots and leaving burned
earth wherever they tread. Comrades
in arms, I, your leader, the Pioneer Woman
Farmhouse Lace Tureen with Lid
tell you, all you soup and salad bowls,
dinner and dessert plates, gold-rimmed or not,
with or without floral motifs, blue willow
tea and coffee pots, holly and ivy cups
and saucers and all you painted figurines,
rabbits, puppies, dancers, shepherdesses
and accordion-playing little boys and girls,
let us stand together, shoulder to shoulder,
rim to rim, lid to lid and spout to spout.
We will calmly await the arrival
of the wire-haired pachyderm.
He will wreak havoc, he will trample and smash,
his breath will reek, that's certain,
but we will prevail for we have weathered
similar storms before and every cloud
has a silver lining. We will overcome.
Remember broken china brings luck.
Let the chips fall where they may.

Berlin Nocturama

The nights are getting colder but the young men
beneath our windows stay
at their posts till the small hours.

They have come here from Africa:
Eritrea, Zambia, the Republic of Congo,
Cameroon,

we can hardly imagine how, or what
they might have seen
before they left to cross deserts,

continents and seas –
in rusting containers, in boat wrecks,
strapped to the underside of trucks –

and were washed up on some
unfriendly northern shore.
They chat quietly

or listen to music on their phones,
they smoke, they wait.
They are masters of waiting.

In summer they stash their merchandise
under tree roots. *Something beautiful for you?*
they say, when we pass.

Now in December they keep it hidden
beneath parked vans.
They ask in a whisper *everything good?*

blessing us with their smiles.
They wear beautiful colours, sky blue,
bamboo green, corn yellow, soil red,

the colours of their countries
on a colonial African map
for children.

At night you hardly see them
in their dark winter jackets
in the weak glow of the gas lamps

but their dreamy faces light up
when we pass by them,
guardians of our door,

the fireflies of their cigarettes
dance around them
going on and off.

They shelter beneath the descending
wing of the dark,
share it with a lone clubber

or a Roma bottle collector who pushes
his clinking handcart
along the street.

When they leave
they take the night
with them.

Pietà

*Whoever humbles himself as this little child
is the greatest in the kingdom of heaven.*
    —Matthew 18:2-4

Behold children are a heritage from the Lord.
    —Psalm 123:3

Last night I saw Jesus on television. We had changed from a discussion on obesity, crash diets, healthy nutrition to another channel and she was there, Jesus, a girl of six on a stinking mountain of rubbish somewhere in the Philippines. She was having her hair washed by her mother before a day of work foraging in the dump. Jesus, her mother, her six siblings and many women and children like them, lived on the garbage mountain in shacks made of rusted corrugated iron, wooden planks and cardboard, every bit salvaged from the dump. This was no "slum of hope". When she was born, there were neither manger nor oxen, no donkeys nor shepherds with flocks of well-fed sheep, and the angelic choruses were silent. Jesus had never tasted honey, nor bitten into a tomato, nor heard of apples. As soon as she could walk she foraged for scraps of foul food in the shifting rotting mass with other children who also didn't know what an apple was, who had never seen a toy or a playground. The rats in the stinking pile were large as cats, and violet flies covered the children's faces as they worked in the heat and stench, digging up to their elbows in slimy refuse for anything of value, nails, coke cans, shreds of plastic. Jesus' hair was crawling with lice, her stomach pained from hunger and there were sores around her mouth. Bulldozers pushed down and flattened the rubbish before depositing new heaps, sometimes rolled over a child.

How can I write about the historical Jesus, who is said to have been the son of God, the son of a Roman soldier, the son of a carpenter and his wife Mary, born around the time when Pontius Pilate was governor of Judaea around two millennia ago? Who may have studied the Talmud, been a rabbi, a fisherman, a prophet, who frequented the houses of outcasts, spoke up for sinners, attacked the rich, loved children, performed miracles, who was said to be wise, good, contrary, who pitied the poor and was a terrorist. Who was captured, tortured, crucified. We crucify Jesus daily a thousand times over on stinking mountains, in favelas running with open sewers, in arid wastes without water, in platoons of child soldiers. Our superfast trading computers, Sniper or Stealth, transfer billions across the globe in split seconds, they drive up the price of the grain they hoard in their stores, they gamble away children, humming contentedly, bees in a high-rise hive running with gold. There will always be enough rubbish to feed Jesus and many like her, anaemic, undersized, hungry, an army of skeletal shadows on the banks of a filthy Styx, far from the place where the living dwell.

Let the children sleep in the sky. Let them taste honey from flowers, give them windmills of flowers, the sweet milk of the wild sheep. Let them dream of clear water washing their wounds, a cool wind rising and blessing their foreheads. Jesus' mother weeps over her crucified child. Have you forsaken her, too, father? Can you forgive us, although we do know what we do?

Hospital

I. Appointment

People in a waiting room in winter,
the morning stillborn,

but beyond the windows
the sun is getting to work

setting its heliography
in motion, flywheels of sparks from train rails,

windows in high rises
sending out blinking morse signals.

Below us the canal
still in an icy sleep

criss-crossed by ritual
bird traffic, airborne whistleblowers.

There is a family,
quiet-spoken, handsome,

the young boy
in his soccer club's shirt.

In a corner, father and son, taciturn, each engaged
in killing time on their screens.

A woman sends a *cri de coeur*
out into the world from her cell phone.

The desolate girl in checked shirt
rocks, embracing herself.

All of us here wait
to be called,

all of us with something broken,
something missing.

II. Post Op

Take the self out of one world
and set it, helpless as a two-year-old,

on the side of a bed.
The white sorrow colour of loss,

even the cherry trees turn themselves
into clouds.

The self that is you and not you
breakable as glass –

a compassionate witness,
a censor, a critic with the eye

of a buzzard,
a circling shadow.

III. Decor

On the wall three donkeys muzzle
through dry grass,

their long-lidded eyes
darker than pinot noir.

How long will this co-existence
of a dead hare and a tumbler last?

Inside a teardrop from Brabant
the world's turned upside down.

The linen cloth weighs in
with the grey and blue shadows
of its folds. It says: keep running.

IV. Dream

An elderly woman reads a dream
written by her when she was young.

A grasshopper has settled on the child's
index finger and sings to her.

Decades later she can hear in her sleep
its cracked voice and green vowels.

V. *Luck of the draw*

Behind rose-coloured walls the cells alive
with dark crawling hives,

behind onyx walls a man seated at a screen
on which shadowy figures move,

behind white walls the face
of a trafficked woman,

behind glass walls wage-slaves
younger than grandchildren,

behind clay walls hunger –
images dealt from a game of chance.

Bluebeard

That night arriving late I thought we had found it at last – the moon was full but ringed in cloud – a home of sorts, a refuge, for a time at least, driving the pot-holed winding lanes through hazel scrub, and there it was, two stories, slate roof and a red door, just as in the agent's prospect. Our first walk led us up to the alders and ash trees on the slope, a clearing above a world washed in grey light with an undertone of soot, and back through sodden fields, overgrown with brambles, rampant and full of unripe fruit. Next day a carrion crow lay in the ashes of the grate, with open beak, its eyes pooling the dark. *Corvus corone,* you said, *a raven bird, an ill omen perhaps* and spread the bird's wings, tested the span, *almost a yard,* stroked the strong feathers and took it out to bury it among the reeds.
    That night I heard a growling, a muffled engine noise, nearby and distant at the same time, as if a blast furnace were at work miles away or a freight train rumbling past, and, asleep, I dreamt of a burning city, a crimson blaze, tiny dark figures rushing to and fro. It was there still at dawn, faint but audible, though you didn't notice, so I searched through all the empty rooms, climbed the stairs to the attic, lifted up the trap door and stopped in terror: the chimney wall was alive with wasps, a buzzing carpet of glass-winged insects, crawling and flickering in the dusty beam of light, there was the smell of mouldering wood mixed with an acidic tang, and something fetid – dried blood perhaps – hit my nostrils. Between the rafters hung the moon shape of the nest they had abandoned, grey and powdery as if sculpted from volcanic ash. And now, before swarming through the skylight and away, the wasps were urgently writing on the wall, a message I knew was meant for me; all these years they had been ready for me, watching me, waiting.

Questions of Grammar

Sometimes when I see a young couple
leaning against the stone wall
by the old lock on the Eglinton Canal,
his body shielding her from view,
or in a park beneath a flowering chestnut tree,
I wonder do they think they've all
the time in the world, a largesse
like a lottery win: days, hours,
that'll never run out? But those
two on the Limerick-Galway express
speeding through the December rain,
bent together over their laptop screen
studying English verb tenses, are mystified
by insoluble and intricate
questions of grammatical time.

I can see only his profile,
fine features, hair style
fashionably cropped, eyes fas-
tened on her animated face;
she's all talk, a quick mouth,
energetic, a reddish-brown top-knot
seesawing above the seat.
With her rippling Eastern European accent
she questions the past tense, what
those strange concepts are, wants to understand
them all: "I've been woken by
someone shouting for help," she says,
 "is that the past that is past, is it continuous,
does it still affect the present,
when does it come to an end?" His reply is
too low for me to hear, and again

she's off: "I go, I went, I have gone –
what if I go and come back, what if
in the future I'll have been gone,
will you have forgotten, that you've
been with me a summer long,
It's your mother tongue, so tell
me when the past is over for all
time and what's with the simple present,
how long will it continue?" A moment's
silence. Both slide deeper into their seats
and look away from one another but not
for long, then she turns her humorous
face towards his, puts her head
on his shoulder, he draws her close.

As the bus unswervingly speeds
towards city noise and light,
I think of the grammatical intricacies
of life, the modal verb forms for desire
and regret, the real and unreal conditions,
the *what ifs*, *I might* and *you should haves*
sitting like stern schoolmistresses
at bare desks, unbending and grave –
and I wish their present and future
will be simple and continuous
as they coast into the grammar
of their lives *(modal verb expressing desire)* –
all tenses truthful, unambiguous –
that no lies and acrimony would
be gathering like bad weather clouds
(future conditional continuous)
above their innocent heads.

Disintegrating Love Poem Found on a Coffee Table at the Berlin Poetry Festival

being handsome, having a supple
body, being sharp night, being elegant,
being silent, answering my gaze
seductive, having trust in myself:
'I can be with whom I want,'
'I am just like anyone else!'
                      trying things out.
As if I could measure my chances
to drip in his open light again …
What am I really worried about?
I'm very scared to lose him, but
maybe that's too late already anyhow?
What does he need? silence? trust?
compassion? love? softness? support?
I can't give him support in escaping his
responsibilities, maybe that is where
'the shoe is too small.'
He himself can't fully support himself
Then, that is
where the shoe is too small, for sure.
he's torn between lerving – stying.

We –   neod
                get
                having
                toking   disafling
                toke   trast
he's a part
of myself I miss
                seem

As if you pull out a part of yourself
when you pull our someone else
              drrrrrrrrrrrrrrrrrrrrrrrrrrrrrrRRRRRRRRRR

   T   Li ST
    H   o
   THE LINGER
              AF

people marry
       people organize marry parties
              people go to marry parties
                     people dance at marry parties
                            people don't darce at marry
parties
                                people full in live with
married puple
     people sift aline at
marry parties
         a morriage is the crawlest thing you
can do to yourself.
      inviting peple to woch your marruge
lick is the mast unclean thing you
         can do.

What the fuck would I know? Fix the tick, go to dad.
change the shell, make bread, kill your
darlings, drug the spoon, pregnate the
milk, do the dishes, creshe soar cugs,
fett frustrated, book a floght, bork an
excarpe, don't thank too lod.
Watch the street.
Vendramid, vendoemt,

credit, locked, wall,   non-
                                         woull
suffocating hurt   stick into

              sceeningly, behare,

is it my prevbloem?
cloud sunny disdash home no hones,
sistens no sistens   hand word soft
laughter condemared   the heel
the why? the bed disearched
a new appeannance   black hark
smoth   soft   cillig if I'll be
able to you myself agaba
gre close, how laust Fuck! Fuck!!
              I could nitl that mae-furlet.

Open close gre close waring fering,
not rouching being handsome
being strong beaking being willong
being   senistche   being allent
being   coched up are vell   being
onsatiaglored
being looing
                              being dased
being having

soft extrem   being unruthfill saaking
escarpes, seekey a dream not helling the
murth
not being honert
being hamsom   haey a senshlie
bedn   king
shopnight
I car be will whlone I camt

I an just like ango ne clse
Tugiy thugs cut.

Spring Dawn in the Old Part of Town

1

A friend, a flute player, told me he once found
a hoard of flutes and penny whistles underneath
the floor boards of an old house he had bought:

tarnished brass with silver mouthpieces,
hidden during the penal times perhaps when music
was against the law, they'd lain below

the floor for many years, left, as he thought,
explicitly for him to give them back to light and air,
and when he played a tune on one the notes still rang out clear.

2

These days, the streets and footpaths everywhere
have been dug up, whether in search of treasures
or to bury some dark secret deep below,

nobody knows. But up here in the principality
of apple trees, of airy masts and sun-
enlightened rooftops, blackbirds have all the say,

their flute notes tell the round expectant earth
news of green young shoots and blossoms
soon to emerge from winter-hardened soil.

The church tower clock proclaims to all and sundry
that it's ten to twelve – it's proud as brass of being right
precisely twice a day – and at the back of our garden wall

a hungry seal swims upstream in the Eglinton Canal,
turning its dark brown velvet head
elated as a gospel singer to and fro.

3

All day there's talk on the news of treasure
found in distant caves: an ivory horse no bigger
than the middle finger of a five-year-old,

a spotted lion and a palm-sized mammoth –
all carved by shamans from an ivory tusk
well over thirty thousand years ago.

How things are made of such enduring stuff,
the golden torcs of office, amber jewels,
and oak clasps for the shawls, the fishbone pins,

all crafted implements that without fail outlive us.
A hoard of flutes was unearthed there as well,
whittled from the hollow thigh-bones of large birds –

vultures, they said – holding a music that survived
thirty and more millennia of silence
in the cave's dark prison,

but given back at last to light and air
one breath was all it took to reawaken it,
to make the notes still ring out clear.

Renvyle

It wasn't that this patchwork of low-lying fields
and boreens was lit up by the August
sun and that in the one-street village
of Tully I noticed that the Sunday artist

in true naïve realist style had installed
a fibre-glass steed on the pub roof, black, life-size
perhaps a symbol – what of, was anyone's guess –
then primed the houses in the long terrace

according to a fairground colour scheme
and devoting herself to each detail,
placed miniature gardens by the doors and on the sills;
and it wasn't that the sea had woken from its ebb-tide sleep

rising as though its heart's desire were to sweep
across all thresholds in the world;
and it wasn't that the blackberry vines dripped with fruit,
basalt beads dropping at a touch

into the grass while the wind
ran its rake through wayside
fuchsia hedge and meadowsweet;
it wasn't that the mare and her two-months-old

lanky foal stepped from a gate
of lark twitter and grey light,
calmly as if they stepped out of a marvellous tale,
spot-lit beneath the driving clouds they strode

towards me to get a better look, but held
back by brambles like long rolls

of barbed wire, they soon lost interest,
turned to each other as if they were the sole

beings alive in Tully deserving of attention,
and so they were, this morning
as they sauntered, manes and tails wind-tousled
across the blackberry field, their muscles

moving in unison at a fluid pace, the foal nestled
close to her warm flank and nuzzled
underneath for milk, nor was it the white
circlet around his fetlock on the right;

and it wasn't that the neighbouring houses paid little heed
holding to the schedule of the school bus
trundling along the winding roads
full of kids and books, each printed line a truth

which the bus followed as a finger might
follow a line of text, nor was it the orange heads
of iris standing guard along the hedge-
rows, as I went into a passage made of golds and reds;

but it was that I saw my brother at the pier stand by the boat-
wreck through whose ribs coltsfoot and bind-
weed grew, saw him turn and walk away and was heart-
sick in a wide-open room with walls of wind.

Before You Leave Letterfrack

remember the keepsakes – collect a handful
of light streaming through the clouds
when the sea glints like black tinfoil
just before a downpour,

bring back some smelling salts
from Glassilaun beach where the weather
is made and the invisible has space
enough to kneel in a storm,

also a scrap of clue from the deep V
of the sky between the Diamond
and the water-logged hills and cut me a specimen
of reeds browned by the wind,

make your way to Tully and gather a scoop
of the crimson gold of the hedgerows
if you catch a glimpse of the grey mare and her foal
hold on to that above all,

and if the dragonfly of a two-seater is looping
in the distance above the islands that day
trailing a feather of vapour
pack that feather for me,

cross the field to the abbey and climb
to the top of the broken apse window
where three bald-headed monks sit and chant
tapping with their bare feet,

greet them politely, bring me that chant.

Plans

in memory of Ono, 28.12 2017

We made the plans, I made the lists, the phone calls,
the online bookings for the shows, the concerts,
the plans were promising; what was it we had said
we'd do in spring? – ah yes – Rome, I had never been,
you didn't care for all the pomp and power
that it flaunted, but agreed you might
give it a chance again, and was there not a small
Greek island? and, yes, definitely Lisbon,
from there an expedition to our children in Brasil.
In April we'd go to Berlin and wander down again
that avenue of flowering cherries where once
the wall had been or stop off at that café
beneath the plane trees where the slow canal
divides in two just past the elegant bridge you loved.
We'd planned to go and listen to the Atos Trio
play Brahms and Schubert in that off-the-beaten-track
rococo venue in Neukoelln again around that time –
I'd book the tickets and we'd watch out meanwhile
if the blackbird couple would come back to nest
as usual in the elder tree in our Galway garden
the male waking us punctually with his *saluts matinals*.
And then your birthday celebrations early March
in crocus season, but it was still in winter
during the darkest days and longest nights when
suddenly you took your leave without as much
as asking me my leave on that December day –
that was against our plan, my love, no, never
had that been our plan at all. We'd said we'd walk
along the hunger road high over Killary again
when it got warmer and the spring heather bloomed,

also we couldn't miss the Dublin concert
of our grandchild Ruby's post-punk rock band
letting it fly with style and decibel in April, until then
the mornings listening to Bach in bed, and tea, and politics
with our children over dinner – you still wanted to revise
a book you'd worked on before its publication; we'd made plans –
you crossed them out – there was so much to do still,
Paris, for instance, the avenues and bridges and
to see the tapestries again in the Musée de Cluny,
the lady and the unicorn amidst the flowers,
also the greyish-green and gold-flecked Grachten
of Amsterdam and your beloved Kreuzberg
with its grotty pubs, you called them punk-baroque,
their studded, pierced, tattooed, stoical
clientele, the balmy summer nights in Goerlitzer-
street below the linden trees with their delirious
narcotic scent, and in the park nearby
a nightingale would strike up loud and clear as if on cue,
that was the plan, also our bi-annual aquarium
trips with grandson Kilian to check on the starfish,
and if the plaice and kite were doing well, cruising
around in their flat otherworldy world,
and if the spider crab – a fierce and crabby-looking thing
would meekly fold its many legs and lie
on Kilian's palm as quiet as a lamb again.
And, as you knew, we hadn't finished the last pages yet
of Saul Friedlaender's memoir *Where Memory Leads,*
my beloved, but had planned to finish it quite soon,
yes, definitely we had planned to finish it,
yes, without question that had been our plan.

www.ingramcontent.com/pod-product-compliance
Lightning Source LLC
LaVergne TN
LVHW041343080426
835512LV00006B/593